THEY DIED TOO YOUNG

ELVIS PRESLEY

Melissa Hardinge

CHELSEA HOUSE PUBLISHERS
Philadelphia

First published in traditional hardback edition
© 1998 by Chelsea House Publishers.
Printed in Hong Kong
Copyright © Parragon Book Service Ltd 1995
Unit 13–17, Avonbridge Trading Estate, Atlantic Road
Avonmouth, Bristol, England BS11 9QD

Illustrations courtesy of Rex Features

Library of Congress Cataloging-in-Publication Data
Hardinge, Melissa.
    Elvis Presley / by Melissa Hardinge.
        p.   cm. — (They died too young)
    Originally published: London: Parragon Books, 1995.
    Includes index.
    Summary: Biography of the "King of Rock 'n' Roll" including
his impoverished childhood, his success as a recording artist,
and his untimely death in 1977.
    ISBN 0-7910-4630-3 (hc)
    1. Presley, Elvis, 1935-1977—Juvenile literature.   2. Rock
musicians—United States—Biography—Juvenile literature.
[1. Presley, Elvis, 1935-1977.   2. Singers.   3. Rock music.]
I. Title.   II. Series.
ML3930.P73H37 1997
782.42166'092—dc21
[B]   97-27574
                                                                CIP
                                                              AC MN

CONTENTS

Elvis the brooding youth

HUMBLE BEGINNINGS

When Elvis Presley died on August 16, 1977, he was the most successful recording artist in the world. He had achieved sixty-three gold singles, twenty-six platinum albums, thirty-seven gold albums, and eighteen number 1 hits. He had been awarded three Grammys, and had starred in thirty-three movies. But his start in life could hardly have been less auspicious.

The Presleys had been down on their luck for generations. Elvis had a great-grandmother who bore ten illegitimate children, and a mad Aunt Dixie who lived in an asylum. The family lived in the poorest part of the small town of Tupelo, Mississippi, and were looked down on by their neighbors.

Vernon Elvis Presley, Elvis's father, was an uneducated laborer; unambitious, idle, and having grown up poor, he did not expect anything different. He got occasional work driving trucks but frittered his wages away on drink and gambling. His mother, Gladys Love Presley (née Smith), was part Cherokee Indian, part Jewish, and part Scots Irish. She worked as a machine operator at the Tupelo Garment Company until Elvis's birth. She had once had dreams of making something of her life, but the Depression and Vernon's waywardness had put a stop to all that. Instead, they were so poor she had to wear rags on her feet instead of shoes, and soon she too began to find that her only escape was in a bottle.

Elvis Aron Presley was born on January 8, 1935, in his parents' tiny two-room shack. Gladys was twenty-two and Vernon was eighteen; they had been married for two years. It was a particularly painful and difficult labor, and Gladys, weak from loss of blood, first gave birth to a stillborn boy, who was later christened Jesse Garon Presley. Thirty-five minutes later, Elvis Aron arrived.

The family could not afford to bury their dead child, so the local church donated a coffin and a plot of land in the cemetery. Tragically, the grave was never marked; when Elvis later wanted to bring his dead brother to be buried at his Graceland home, he was unable to find him.

Gladys was distraught at her loss, and became inconsolable when told she would not be able to have more children. She clung hysterically to her surviving son, not letting even Vernon near him. The family gilded Jesse's memory. Gladys would use his death to discipline the young Elvis: "Jesse would never have treated his Mama like that." And Elvis would always think of Jesse as his other half—he could never be whole until he was reunited with him in the hereafter. "If only Jesse were here," he would say whenever something good happened.

When Elvis was three, Vernon was arrested for forging a $100 check. During his time in prison Gladys and Elvis were homeless and would walk to the benefit office through the snow with bare feet, setting the uncharitable tongues of Tupelo wagging.

Gladys's one consolation was Elvis; she adored her pretty child with his blond hair and big blue eyes. In Vernon's absence, a powerful bond grew between mother and son, and when Vernon was released from prison eight months later, pleading family hardship, he found his wife haggard, exhausted, and completely unreceptive to him.

6   *They Died Too Young*

While Vernon was unlikely to want to better himself and Gladys knew her own lot was probably fixed, she was determined that her only child would have every chance to improve himself: perhaps he would one day have a steady job with a pension, maybe even one day he would be a preacher. She walked her son to school every day, and made sure they attended church regularly—a Pentecostal chapel with wild euphoric services. Elvis apparently loved going, and would squirm on his mother's knee or run up the aisle whenever the hymns were played.

Gladys was anxious to ensure that her son would have the decency and integrity so lacking in his father. One day eight-year-old Elvis was walking back from school with his cousin, when they passed a farmer selling apples. Determined to get one for Gladys and knowing he had no money, he sneaked around the back of the truck and took one off the back. But when he presented it to his mother, she marched him all the way back to the farmer, handed back the apple, and made him apologize. Elvis later said that the incident would never have happened had they not been so poor, and it only strengthened his determination to get rich so he could give his beloved mother everything Vernon had failed to provide.

From the age of ten, Elvis worked to bring in money for the family. During one period, when both his parents were unemployed, he worked after school doing odd jobs every evening from 3 to 10 P.M. For his tenth birthday, Gladys bought him a guitar (the bicycle he wanted was too expensive) and his uncle showed him a few chords. He would sit for hours copying the songs on the radio, everything from the blues and gospel to hillbilly and pop.

The biggest event of the year in the South was the Mississippi–Alabama Fair, and the highlight for the people of Tupelo and the surrounding towns was the talent contest. Gladys persuaded Elvis to enter. Shaking with nerves, he had to stand on a chair to reach the microphone, but his rendition of "Old Shep" brought the house down and he won the second prize of five dollars. Gladys wept with pride—she said it was the best day of her whole life—and Elvis rather enjoyed his first taste of public approval.

When Elvis was thirteen, the family was forced to move to Memphis, Tennessee, because Vernon had been caught moonshining (making whisky illegally) and was run out of town by the county sheriff. Elvis was furious at his father for letting them down yet again, this time so publicly, but Vernon promised he would try to get a steady job in Memphis and the family began to see the move as a fresh start.

Elvis found it difficult to adjust to the bustle of a big city. He missed the countryside of Tupelo and he hated his new school, which was enormous (fifteen hundred pupils). On the first day he walked straight home after Vernon dropped him off. And Gladys would not let him try out for the football team because she was afraid he might get hurt.

Meanwhile there was barely enough money to live on, and the relationship between Vernon and Gladys disintegrated as they bickered in their tiny apartment. Elvis helped out doing odd jobs, mowing lawns and delivering milk. When things were really bad he would sell a pint of blood to the local hospital for a few dollars. He bitterly resented the fact that it seemed to be his responsibility to support the family, not Vernon's. He would run down the street until he wore himself out, or smash the windows of deserted tenement blocks.

In the spring of 1949 they became desperate, and Elvis begged to be allowed to leave school so he could earn more money. But if Gladys and Vernon agreed about anything, it was that their son needed an education, and Gladys continued to walk him to school until he persuaded her not to. Even then she followed one block behind.

Eventually they swallowed their pride, applied for welfare, and were moved to a housing project in a largely

They Died Too Young

As a young rocker

Just one of Elvis's Cadillacs

black area. Elvis was still unhappy in school, but he was used to being an outsider and spent a lot of time on his own, wandering around downtown Memphis. He would hang around the blues clubs on Beale Street and at Lansky's where the black musicians bought their flashy clothes, and listen to the gospel choirs in the churches on the black side of town. He dyed his long blond hair black, and greased it up like a helmet. He bought bright-colored second-hand clothes—pink shirts with green trousers, polka dots with stripes—and he even wore mascara to cover up his blond eyelashes (Gladys's idea). "At least it'll be easy to spot me if I get run over," he said.

And he discovered girls. First it was a shy crush on one of the usherettes at the cinema where he had a holiday job. Then it was a succession of Saturday night dates he would take to the movies. Gladys hated the idea of sharing her son and made Elvis feel as guilty as possible when he was just about to go out. Elvis's first true love was Dixie Locke, who sat opposite him in English class. She was everything Elvis dreamed of, sweet and kind; he could not believe a girl like that could be interested in him. He even plucked up enough courage to tell her he lived in the projects, and was convinced she must love him when her only response was to rock him gently in her arms.

With newfound confidence, Elvis entered the Humes High senior class variety show, in which he sang a ballad. He won, to the astonishment of his classmates. For the first time Elvis felt invincible. He was going to be a famous singer. He would be able to buy Gladys anything she wanted. And he would marry Dixie. But when Elvis proposed to her on their senior prom night, Dixie said no. Elvis could not believe it, and spent the next weeks moping around and crying, completely disillusioned. Gladys could hardly disguise her relief.

The smoldering looks that won a million hearts

SAM PHILLIPS AND COLONEL PARKER

In the summer of 1953 Elvis graduated, the first Presley to finish high school. Still heartbroken, he busied himself with trying to find work, signing up at the unemployment center. He needed to find a well-paid job, because Gladys was confined to her bed with a mysterious illness and Vernon was happy to let Elvis assume the burden of bringing home the daily bread. First he worked at the factory of the Precision Tool Company, then he was taken on as a driver for Crown Electric, for $45 a week.

Working only forty hours a week, Elvis had more free time than he had ever known. He was drawn to Beale Street and would sit for hours in the smoky clubs, listening to the music and meeting women who were altogether different from his high school sweetheart. He was determined never to let a woman hurt him again.

Elvis's first public performance after high school was at Hernando's Hideaway, a seedy bar where they jeered at his green trousers and pink shirt. Even though he had a bottle thrown at him that night, he persevered, and over the next few months he searched out every amateur night and talent competition in the Memphis area. It was grueling and depressing, and more than once he came close to quitting.

Late in the summer of 1953, Elvis set foot in a recording studio for the first time. He had seen the sign "We record anything, anytime, anywhere, $3 one side, $4 two sides" in the window of Sam Phillips's Memphis Recording Service, also the base for the Sun record label. The story goes that Elvis wanted to make a record as a birthday present for his mother. But as his mother's birthday was in April, it seems more likely that he just wanted to hear how he sounded on vinyl.

The studio was very busy that afternoon. While he was waiting, the receptionist, Marion Keisker, tried to strike up a conversation with him. "Who do you sound like?" she asked. "I don't sound like nobody, ma'am," he replied. Marion was sufficiently interested to stick a tape in a spare machine when his turn came. She knew that the owner of Sun Records, Sam Phillips, was looking for a new star, having previously launched the careers of Roy Orbison and Jerry Lee Lewis. Phillips is famously quoted as saying that he knew that if he could find a white man who could sing with the sound of a black man, then he could make a billion dollars.

When Marion played him the first tape, he liked it but was not overwhelmed. Apparently he thought nothing more of it until Elvis showed up at the studio again the following January (1954) to make a record for a girlfriend. This time Phillips was at the controls himself, was considerably more impressed, and took a contact number (the rabbi who lived downstairs from the Presleys, who did not have a phone).

When Elvis returned home from work a few weeks later to find a message that Sun Records had called, he immediately assumed it was the receptionist being forward. But when he phoned he discovered, to his utter disbelief, that it was Sam Phillips who wanted to speak to him. Apparently Phillips did not necessarily think that Elvis was "the one," but he needed a singer to record a ballad called "Without You." The song had originally been sent to him on a demo tape, and they could not find the singer, an unknown kid who had just happened to be hanging around the studio.

But Elvis's enthusiasm could not make up for his lack of

experience. "Without You" was a difficult song, and even though they tried it again and again, the results were disastrous. Elvis was mortified, becoming more and more choked with every take. Then, during a break, Phillips asked Elvis what he could sing. He took a deep breath, and gave it everything he had: gospel hymns, blues songs, Dean Martin covers, sometimes a snatch of a chorus, sometimes the whole song.

Phillips decided to give him a second chance, and he introduced him to two musicians: Scotty Moore, a twenty-one-year-old guitarist, and Bill Black, a bassist. Together they experimented and rehearsed, performing at a couple of clubs, then going back into the studio. None of them really knew the sound they were looking for; it was not regimented Bill Haley country-swing, nor was it straight country, or straight rhythm & blues, or straight pop. Then during a break on the night of July 5, 1954, Elvis suddenly started singing an old country blues track, "That's All Right, Mama," and when the two musicians improvised and joined in, Phillips knew they were on to something. They recorded the track, and put "Blue Moon of Kentucky" on the B side.

Just two days later, as a favor to Phillips, the biggest Memphis radio station, WHBQ, agreed to play the record. Elvis was too nervous to listen to it, so he tuned his parents' radio for them and left to go to see a Tony Curtis movie at the local movie theater. Within a week, Sun had received over five thousand orders for the record. It climbed to number 3 on the local country and western chart, but even though Phillips mailed copies to every big national radio station, it dropped like a stone.

Meanwhile Elvis carried on working at the Crown Electric. Although he, Scotty, and Bill were doing more night-club dates, he was reluctant to give up the security of the truck-driving job. Only when Phillips gave him his first royalty check, for $200, did Elvis finally hand in his keys. His first purchases were a dress and a pair of shoes for Gladys.

Her feet were far too swollen to fit into the shoes, but she kept them in a plastic bag at the side of her bed, and would look at them every time she passed the door.

As Elvis began to pick up bookings away from home, Phillips impressed upon him the importance of getting a manager. He had the studio and label to run and could no longer give Elvis's career the attention it needed. He suggested a local DJ, Bob Neal, and even though Vernon was unimpressed, Elvis liked his friendly style. Gladys and Vernon signed the contract on their son's behalf (Elvis was under age), but neither side had a lawyer present. That oversight would cost Neal dearly.

Neal set to work improving Elvis's image. He arranged for him to have a new Chevrolet on credit, and encouraged him to wear black on stage—he thought the bright colors distracted from Elvis's singing. He even had the warts burnt off Elvis's hands.

In January 1955 Elvis released his second record, "Good Rockin' Tonight," but it was greeted with only modest enthusiasm, and his third single, "Milkcow Blues" did even less well. It seemed that the novelty of the first record had worn off, and certain town councils and church meetings started to object to the "animalistic" music. Local DJs got the message and did not play the records.

In May 1955 twenty-year-old Elvis went on a three-week tour. He looked incredibly handsome, he moved suggestively, and for the first time he had his shirt, his jacket, even his shoes ripped off him by screaming girls. Standing in the shadows at these performances was someone who within a year would make this teenage hysteria a national phenomenon.

Colonel Tom Parker was not really a colonel, nor was Tom Parker his real name. He was actually Dries Van Kuijk, a Dutch illegal immigrant whose conflicting ambitions were to be fantastically rich, but not be traced by the immigration authorities. He was already managing some minor country stars, but when he recognized Elvis,

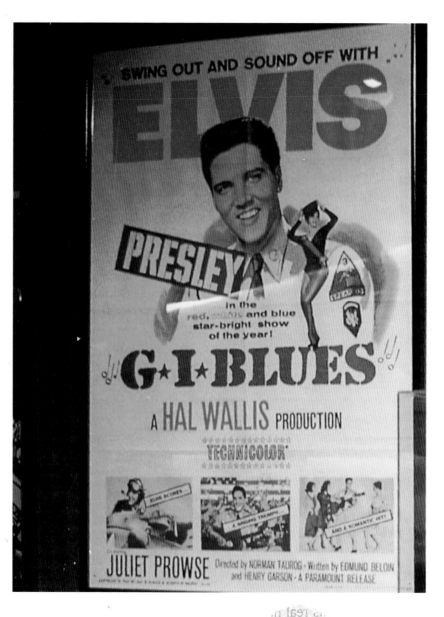

One-sheet movie poster for the film GI Blues

he saw the potential that Phillips and Neal had both missed.

Parker knew that the way to Elvis was through his mother, so he introduced himself to Vernon and Gladys at a club, saying how proud they must be that their son was only months away from huge success. Vernon took to him instantly, and when Parker offered to act as Elvis's consultant, Vernon was all for accepting, even though Gladys said he made her skin crawl. Elvis was not sure what a consultant was, but he desperately wanted his records to break through into the mainstream, and he thought Parker might well be able to help.

White rhythm and blues was a revolution waiting to happen. Parker knew that Elvis could be the leader, and gradually he set about increasing his control over Elvis's career. Through his connections he got Elvis bookings at larger venues, and the next single, "Baby Let's Play House," broke through into the national country music chart. Then Parker made his move. He took the family out to a posh restaurant and set about expressing his concerns that Elvis's present management did not have what it took to go all the way to the top. He said that with all his connections, he could get Elvis a record deal with one of the big record companies inside a month.

The Presleys went home that night and had a long discussion. Vernon was utterly convinced that they needed Parker, while Gladys completely mistrusted him. Elvis was worried about offending Neal and Phillips, the people who had first believed in him. "If it weren't for Mr. Phillips, I'd still be driving a truck." But his desire to be somebody eventually got the better of his qualms: he signed with Parker. It would be a 50–50 split.

Parker's first move was to sell Elvis to the highest bidder. They saw every major record company in New York, and eventually chose the biggest fish in the pond, RCA. Phillips got a $35,000 payoff (which he later invested in a new Memphis business called Holiday Inn), Neal got nothing and Elvis received a check for $5,000. It was money beyond his wildest dreams. Within weeks, the family moved into their own house, for once on the right side of town, and Vernon and Gladys gave up any attempt at working. At last Elvis could afford to buy himself suits straight from Lansky's, and even take girls out on dates at Memphis's best restaurants.

A fan with Elvis memorabilia

"CORRUPTING THE NATION'S YOUTH"

Elvis made his first recordings for RCA in Nashville two days after his twenty-first birthday in January 1956. "Heartbreak Hotel" was released two weeks after it was recorded and it rocketed up the *Billboard* charts. "Don't Be Cruel," "Hound Dog," and "I Want You, I Need You, I Love You" soon followed, and the poor only child from the wrong side of town suddenly became the hottest singer in America.

Parker knew the power of the media, and the publicity that could be gained from a bit of healthy controversy, so he paid dozens of girls to faint at Elvis's performances in early 1956. America's youth were only too ready to respond to an idol they could relate to, and his appeal increased in direct proportion to their parents' disapproval. Rock 'n' roll was here to stay, and America had never seen anything like it.

Elvis himself was a bit dazed too. "Everything's happened so fast in the past year and a half, I'm all mixed up," he said. The one thing he did appreciate was the importance of the music; he insisted on doing thirty takes of "Hound Dog" because he wanted it to be perfect. But he was also starting to feel the strain of his double life: on stage he was the sexy star surrounded by adoring women, but he was a plain old mama's boy when he got home.

Gladys had more jewelry and clothes than at any time in

her life, but she felt neglected now that Elvis was spending more time away from her than he had ever done. Plus her new neighbors became argumentative when she wanted to build a chicken coop in her backyard. She turned to the bottle with a vengeance.

Meanwhile, the Colonel encouraged his young charge to be utterly dependent on him. He would explain financial arrangements in the most complicated terms, and when Elvis did not understand, the Colonel would pat him on the back and tell him just to worry about the singing. When the record company was trying to write a sanitized biography of their new star, Elvis confided in the Colonel about Vernon's disreputable past. Parker reassured Elvis that no one would find out, and stored up the information for his own use later. But even though Elvis did not like Parker personally, he certainly liked what was happening to his career. "Hey, I'll stick with anyone who'll make me rich," he declared.

Television was the next step, bringing the raw energy of Elvis's performance straight into the living rooms of middle-class America. Elvis appeared on the Dorsey Brothers Stage Show, singing "Heartbreak Hotel," and though the performance was well received, he could not wait to leave New York—he was fed up with people teasing him about his "cute" Southern accent.

As Elvis's career took off, so did the backlash against him. His performance of "Hound Dog" on Milton Berle's TV show caused outrage, and journalists asked him how he felt about corrupting the morals of the nation's youth. He said that moving to the music came naturally to him, and that he did not see the harm in it. He also hated the phrase on everyone's lips, "Elvis the Pelvis." "It's one of the most childish expressions I ever heard coming from an adult," he complained in interviews.

The Colonel had to act quickly to prevent these criticisms from gaining momentum, and set about taming his star. First came elocution lessons, and then, in July 1956, he

They Died Too Young

made him appear on the *Steve Allen Show* in a tuxedo and sing his hit "Hound Dog" to a basset hound wearing a top hat. Elvis was furious and humiliated, but as usual he did as he was told.

Though Elvis was controversial, even disliked, he was news, and by September 1956 it was worth an unprecedented $50,000 to *The Ed Sullivan Show* to have him appear. Some fifty-four million people tuned into the show that night, an 82 percent share of the audience. Even though Ed Sullivan told the audience that Elvis was a "real decent fine boy," CBS insisted he only be filmed from the waist up. Such censorship only served to increase Elvis's notoriety, and that night Elvis gyrated with everything that was visible.

From television, the next stop had to be movies. Parker negotiated a deal with Hollywood film producer Hal Wallis, who had spotted Elvis's potential at a show in Vegas, and Elvis was cast as Flint Reno in *Love Me Tender*. The film was critically panned, but the audiences loved it and flocked to see it. Whether Elvis had any talent as an actor is a moot point, but the fact that he had to make four movies over the next eighteen months hardly gave him any chance to learn the craft. *Love Me Tender* (1956) was followed by *Loving You* (1957), *Jailhouse Rock* (1957) and *King Creole* (1958), all tapping into the poor-boy-makes-good mythology that was Elvis's own story.

The Colonel was not interested in high art—he wanted to see results from his time and commitment. Even though Elvis was offered parts in movies playing opposite Burt Lancaster and Tony Curtis, Parker was happier to accept scripts where there was no doubt who was the star. This concept applied to Elvis's records too: there was little choice of material, because Parker had tied Elvis to singing songs from one particular publishing house. Parker also had no qualms about approving as "official" Elvis merchandise everything from tacky stuffed hound dogs to pajamas, without any regard to their quality.

The army was good for the image

THE DRAFT

Elvis did not take easily to Hollywood. He fell desperately in love with his first costar, Debra Paget, then with another young starlet, Natalie Wood. His parents had joined him in Los Angeles, and even though Vernon had no problem with going off sightseeing, Gladys remained stubbornly at Elvis's side, even on the set. This meant that Elvis's usual recreational activities had to be curtailed, and he spent long hours cooped up in his hotel room, driving room service crazy with orders for peanut butter sandwiches and ice cream in the middle of the night.

When Elvis went home between his movies, Las Vegas appearances, and TV shows, his local celebrity and the crush of fans waiting at the gates of his house made him review his living arrangements. First he hired an old school friend, Red West, as a bodyguard, then he set about finding the family a new home.

Graceland was set on a wide leafy street in an area of Memphis called White Haven. The property had fourteen rooms and enough space in the grounds for Gladys to have chickens without the neighbors complaining. Such a home, costing $100,000, was suitable for rich businessmen and diplomats—not bad for people who had once been too poor to buy shoes. He moved the whole family in July 1957, plus his Grandma Minnie Mae and some cousins and friends for good measure. Graceland represented everything he had aspired to. He even had the outside repainted so that his Memphis neighbors could see it glowing in the dark.

Red became Elvis's constant companion, and soon there was a group of men, some on the payroll, with whom he would hang out. As a perpetual outsider, Elvis now relished his role as ringleader. When he was at home he would rent the local amusement park or the skating rink for the evening and would stay up until dawn with his friends and their dates. He felt happier when he was with his entourage, and rarely ventured outside Graceland without company. He would go out with Red, looking for dates, and—since he could not take a girl back to Graceland in case Gladys found out—he would always make sure he was back by dawn.

The first Christmas at Graceland was a lavish affair. Elvis even got up at noon (early by his standards) in honor of the celebration. He showered everyone with presents, lit up Graceland like a Christmas tree, and swigged champagne by the bottle. It would be the last truly happy family holiday.

Elvis was now dating a Memphis television presenter, Anita Wood, though he still continued to see other women. But others—especially Vernon—thought they should make the relationship permanent. Early in 1958, when Elvis was watching her on TV, he suddenly saw a close-up of a ring on her hand—a ring he had given her the week before. Elvis flew into a rage, screaming that she was only interested in him for his money. This was a frequent complaint; Elvis loved to be generous, but he was always suspicious that people were only friendly because of his success. He was proud when his old classmates would call on him, and was only too pleased to show off the house, but when they had gone he would berate them, saying that when he had been in their class at school they would have nothing to do with him.

The year 1958 was a whirlwind of recording commitments and concerts. But in March, midway through filming

Graceland

his fourth movie, the bombshell dropped. The Colonel called to say that Elvis had been drafted into the army. Elvis was in a state of disbelief and had a panic attack, hurling furniture out of the window of the expensive Beverly Hills hotel where he was staying. He thought it was the Presley curse, coming once again when things were going so well.

Elvis was frantic at the thought of being away from the music scene for two whole years—what if everyone forgot about him and he had to go back to playing small-town clubs on his return? The Colonel reassured him that they had a movie and several singles ready to go, and that maybe absence would make the teenage hearts clamor for him even more on his return.

Elvis left for Fort Hood training camp in Texas, getting his famous black haircut shorn in full view of the cameras. The family followed two weeks later to a nearby house in Killeen—not living on base was the one concession Elvis was allowed. Elvis hated the army—he had always hated being told what to do, and he missed his music and his girlfriends. His body ached from the arduous workouts and long hours, and he felt a constant pressure not to make a fool of himself in front of the other soldiers.

Meanwhile, the heat in Texas was getting to Gladys. Her skin had turned yellow, and after a few months the family was so concerned about her health that Vernon agreed to take her back to Memphis to see a trusted doctor. While Elvis was fearful for her, he was secretly relieved that she was going home, because it meant he could invite in some of the pretty young fans who hung around outside the house.

Diagnosed with hepatitis, Gladys was kept for a few days in the Memphis City Methodist Hospital, where Elvis called her constantly. Though she was only forty-five she was over-weight and in very poor health, her liver swollen from years of drinking. She did not respond to the medications, and her condition deteriorated so much that Vernon arranged for Elvis to have compassionate leave to come see her. For once

Elvis overcame his fear of flying and rushed to be with her. He was shocked by his mother's appearance, but Gladys insisted that he go home to Graceland to get some rest before coming back to see her the next morning. He went out, hung out with some friends, and then went to his room with Anita.

Gladys died in the middle of the night of August 14, 1958. It was Vernon who broke the news to Elvis, who froze with the shock, sobbing, inconsolable, and furious with himself that he had not stayed at the hospital to be with her at the end. As the news of her death broke, a huge crowd gathered outside Graceland, and there were hundreds of messages of condolence. Even Dixie, Elvis's first love, showed up at the house, and he just hugged and hugged her. He found no comfort with Anita—he felt guilty that he had been with her when Gladys was taking her last breaths.

The funeral on August 16 was the worst day of Elvis's life. When the attendants came to take the body away (it had been laid out in the music room), Elvis leapt on top of the coffin crying uncontrollably, "Don't leave me mama. I did everything for you. I'll do better this time, just let me try."

Gladys's death fundamentally changed Elvis. He never forgave himself for letting her down, and he never forgave her for leaving him and going to Jesse, her favorite son. The main focus of his life was gone, and from that point on, he was on a collision course with disaster.

The day after the funeral he had to return to Texas. To dull the pain, he now surrounded himself with people. Whereas before he had not wanted to befriend his fellow officers, he now began to invite them over for meals and drinking, seeking out those who would cater to his every whim. He began to have trouble sleeping, and would have people on guard to make sure he did not sleepwalk out of the house.

In September 1958 Elvis was shipped with his division to Bad Nauheim in West Germany. He was pleasantly surprised that his fame preceded him, and that German fans allowed him a little more privacy than their American counterparts. He brought Vernon, Red West, and Grandma Minnie Mae over, and they moved into a comfortable three-bedroom house, with a piano, television sets, and refrigerators full of hamburgers.

Back in the United States, the Colonel worked hard to keep Elvis's career alive. He ran Elvis Presley competitions, where the prize was visiting Elvis in Germany, and sanctioned a "fanzine" called *Elvis Monthly*. Both the *Loving You* and *King Creole* albums went platinum, and singles like "One Night," "Wear My Ring Around Your Neck," and "Hard Headed Woman" went straight into the top 10. Elvis's recording career was now so strong that the 1959 edition of the *Guinness Book of World Records* listed him as overtaking Bing Crosby as the most successful singer of all time.

In Germany a thousand fan letters would arrive at the local post office every day. Meanwhile Elvis busied himself with sampling German nightlife, and even flew some of his "Memphis Mafia" over for excursions to Paris and Munich. Then he met Priscilla.

Priscilla Beaulieu was the daughter of an air force captain, and she was introduced to Elvis at a party at his house. "Well, what have we here?" he said. One of his friends had spotted her in a cafe and thought that Elvis might like her. Her parents had only allowed her to go when her father realized that he knew the commanding officer of the man concerned.

Priscilla knew who Elvis was. Like every other fan she had bought his records and watched him on television. When they were introduced, she was so nervous she could hardly speak, but her reserve attracted him, and she was invited back. What struck Elvis was the resemblance he thought she bore to photographs of the young Gladys. He thought that Jesse had sent Gladys back to him in the form of Priscilla, and almost immediately he put her right up there on the pedestal next to his mother. He liked the fact that she was only fourteen—young and pure, unlike those other women who were after him all the time.

Elvis began to want to see Priscilla all the time. But her parents insisted that they meet him before they were prepared to let this happen. Elvis dressed up in his uniform for the occasion and charmed the Beaulieus with his lovely manners. They agreed that the couple could carry on seeing each other if Elvis promised he would drop Priscilla off personally after each date. Elvis agreed. In the few remaining months of Elvis's service they saw each other practically every night.

Elvis returned home to Memphis on March 2, 1960, and was discharged from the army three days later. Priscilla accompanied him to the airport, and later the papers were full of the story of the girl he left behind. Priscilla declined to be flown over to the States to appear on television shows, and tried to be evasive about her age when nosy journalists became too curious.

Elvis and Priscilla

PRISCILLA

Elvis had not been forgotten while he was away. He was besieged by fans at the airport, and the Colonel drew up a busy schedule for him, with the intention of plunging him straight back into the spotlight. Plans were made for the next movie (hardly surprisingly, *G.I. Blues*). Vegas wanted him for a concert stint, and Elvis could hardly wait to get started. But events at home put a damper on the triumphant return to which he had looked forward.

Vernon announced to Elvis that he was in love with Dee Stanley, a pretty blonde woman twenty years his junior, and he planned to marry her after her divorce from her present husband was finalized. Elvis was outraged. He had often not seen eye to eye with his father, but this was the ultimate betrayal. He himself had not begun to come to terms with the death of his mother and was shocked that his father could even contemplate another woman. He refused to go to their wedding, and when Vernon moved Dee into Graceland, he kept out of their way as much as he could, throwing himself into his work.

However, he quickly became disillusioned with that too. He thought the *G.I. Blues* script was terrible, and could not believe the cynicism of the studio in wanting to cash in on his time in the service. Evidently the aim of the film was to make soldiering seem fun; hence Elvis was to be the patriotic all-American ideal. It was a far cry from the scandalous rebel that American teenagers had taken to their hearts.

When he went back into the studio in Nashville, he found that the songs RCA wanted him to record were disappointing, middle-of-the-road ballads. "Stuck on You," "Are You Lonesome Tonight?" and "It's Now or Never" were all massive hits but could hardly be described as rock 'n' roll, and segments of the press began to criticize him for cashing in on his success. His appearance on a Frank Sinatra TV special, in his uniform and then a tuxedo, confirmed these suspicions. Elvis expressed his concerns to Parker, but the Colonel was adamant: Elvis had to do the work to reestablish himself on the American music scene. Again Elvis passively agreed.

Over the next nine years, Elvis made twenty-six films. The most memorable of these were *Blue Hawaii* (1961) with Angela Lansbury, *Girls! Girls! Girls!* (1962), *Viva Las Vegas* (1964) with Ann-Margret, and *A Change of Habit* (1969) with Mary Tyler Moore. Elvis hated them all without exception. He may have been paid a million dollars a movie, but this left no spare money for nice sets, good directors, or worthy actors, and he felt embarrassed by the corny scripts and painful plotlines. But the Colonel was happy because Elvis was Hollywood's highest-paid star; the studio was happy because not one of the movies made a loss; and RCA was happy because it could release an album off the back of each movie.

At home in 1962 Elvis felt isolated, restless, and moody. He moved more friends into Graceland and would keep them busy with errands at all hours of the day and night. He gorged himself on junk food, then starved himself before each movie, and he gobbled pills like they were candy. He was angry with Gladys for leaving him, angry with Vernon and Dee, angry with his hangers-on for sponging off him.

There seemed to be only one way out of his depression.

With some of the cast of Blue Hawaii

He sent for Priscilla. It was nearly two years since he had left Germany; Priscilla was now sixteen, and after a tremendous battle with her parents to let her go, she arrived, petrified that Elvis might find fault with her. But Elvis thought she was perfect. He took her shopping and dressed her up in the latest fashions.

It went so well that she was invited back for Christmas. He gave her a poodle puppy and she gave him a cigarette case that played "Love Me Tender." The whole house seemed to be uplifted by her laughter, and Elvis was briefly transformed into the Elvis of old. He decided that he was not going to let her go back to Germany, and he phoned her parents on New Year's Day 1963.

The deal they struck was that Priscilla would return to Germany to finish her school year. She would then move to Memphis, stay as a guest of Vernon and Dee, and attend the local high school. In the autumn of 1963 she enrolled at an all-girls school, the Immaculate Conception. With Priscilla safely installed, not to say imprisoned, at Graceland, Elvis continued making movies, recording albums, and chasing women. Every time he went to Hollywood, the papers would link him to Nancy Sinatra or his other costars, and for the most part the stories were true. Elvis would deny it to Priscilla, and his friends were given strict instructions not to let on.

The tension between them grew, but Priscilla always backed down from challenging him too hard because she wanted only to please him. She would do everything for him, from checking that the maids had prepared his food the way he liked it, to agreeing to dye her hair black so it matched his. She cheated on her finals tests and graduated, and Elvis gave her a red Corvair, her first car.

Priscilla now thought that she would be able to spend all her time with Elvis, but she was wrong. She became frustrated with his absences and with the second home he had set up in Palm Springs, California. Elvis could not believe that a girl in her position could possibly complain. But all she wanted was for him to pay her a bit of attention.

Elvis's mood swings and depression returned. He took more and more pills, and he had sudden flashes of anger and would yell at Priscilla for the slightest thing. In his spare time he would constantly change hobbies; when it was not horses, it was yoga, or karate, or Bible readings, or simply staring at the stars for hours at a time. He would even go and visit the Memphis morgue at midnight—he loved the way his fame could open any door.

By 1965 record sales were down, and audiences began to tire of seeing endless movies with apparently the same plot. Elvis had not made a TV appearance since the Sinatra special in 1960, and his last number 1 had been back in the spring of 1962. His fans were still loyal, but he no longer captured the hearts of America's youth—The Beatles and The Rolling Stones were doing that, and Elvis was considered a little passé. Elvis took this hard: he had always needed the adoration of his fans to feel lovable as a person. Even in the studio, where he had always been in control, the technicians were starting to listen to the record company bosses, not to him.

In 1966 Elvis released just four singles, and only one, "Love Letters," managed to scrape into the top 20. The next year was even more disastrous in terms of record sales, and his albums met with public indifference. Elvis may have been putting less work into the records, but the material he was being offered was simply not original, and now all the best songwriters were performers themselves. Once the rebel who shocked the world, Elvis was now firmly part of the status quo, and Colonel Parker did not have the imagination to see that he could compete, vainly hoping that the new fad would just go away.

The new blood, however, did recognize that Elvis had paved the way for them. John Lennon was quoted as saying, "Before there was Elvis, there was nothing." When The

Beatles came to America, they hung out with Elvis for an afternoon, playing pool and singing. But Elvis said later in an interview that they were "subversive"; perhaps he forgot that the same word had been used against him just a decade earlier.

The pressure was mounting on Elvis to make his relationship with Priscilla official. He was reluctant: he liked the idea that his fans thought he might be available, and also if he was not technically married then he would not technically be cheating on Priscilla if he strayed. However, a messy affair with Ann-Margret, when he was filming *Fun in Acapulco* in 1966, propelled him toward marriage. He did not want to have to deal with the strong egos of Hollywood women, and he mistakenly thought that he could still mold Priscilla into his ideal woman. And the Colonel persuaded him that the public would not stand for Priscilla living at Graceland unmarried much longer.

Just before Christmas 1966 Elvis proposed to Priscilla at Graceland, and they were married in Las Vegas in the full glare of maximum publicity on May 1, 1967. For their brief honeymoon they flew in Frank Sinatra's jet to Palm Springs, with the ever-present "Memphis Mafia" in tow. Within weeks Elvis was back to the old routine, womanizing in Palm Springs, while Priscilla waited for him at Graceland. Even the news that she was pregnant did not make him change.

Lisa Marie Presley, Elvis's sole heir, was born on February 1, 1968. She had lots of silky black hair, and Elvis was delighted with her, though he did not take on a practical role as father. And Elvis and Priscilla grew further and further apart.

Elvis and Priscilla were married in May 1967

The new-look Elvis in the rhinestone suit

FINAL CHALLENGES

In January 1968 Elvis recorded "U.S. Male," which went to number 28 in March, his biggest hit in two years. He was itching to perform again and, for once, the Colonel agreed, putting out the word that Elvis was making a "comeback." Elvis was infuriated by the notion, and said that the only reason people might think that he had been away was the lousy movies that the Colonel had made him do.

Elvis in fact wanted to do a world tour—to go to Europe and Japan (he had never performed outside America before), but the Colonel would not hear of it. Elvis did not know about the problems the Colonel would have coming back into the country if he left. Instead Parker negotiated a deal for an hour-long Christmas special on NBC in 1968 for a $500,000 fee. The Colonel envisioned Elvis dressed in a black tuxedo, singing a few carols like Perry Como and Andy Williams. Elvis had other ideas. The special, his first TV appearance since 1960, would be a chance to reestablish himself as a rock 'n' roll singer.

The young producer of the show also wanted to challenge him. To reinforce the cruel truth that Elvis was not as hot as he used to be, he took him on a stroll in broad daylight down a crowded street on Sunset Strip, and Elvis felt suitably humbled when hardly a head turned in his direction.

He got to work, lost forty pounds, and worked with a whole new range of producers and musicians. On the night of the show, dressed in black leather from head to foot, he sang with all the conviction of his genius. The specially written song "If I Can Dream" was a fitting climax, and he got rapturous applause. Elvis was jubilant afterward, though he had to be cut out of his suit since his sweat had stuck to the leather.

In the aftermath of the concert, Elvis's record sales improved. "If I Can Dream" reached number 12, and the soundtrack album of the concert, *Elvis*, got to number 8. Musically, 1969 saw Elvis challenged again, and he recorded arguably some of his best work with his new, deeper, mellower voice. He cut three top ten singles "In the Ghetto," "Don't Cry Daddy," and "Suspicious Minds" (his last number 1). The tracks were not rock 'n' roll, nor were they blues, but rather mature pop.

In December 1970 Elvis pulled his most bizarre stunt yet. He flew to Washington, without an appointment, determined to see President Nixon. Wearing a black velvet suit and cape, he was received in the Oval office, and told Nixon that he wanted to work for him in the fight against drugs. The president was rather taken aback but gave Elvis a Narcotics Bureau badge, and the new "agent" went back to Graceland beaming with pride.

The Colonel had kept Elvis from touring for a decade because he had not figured out how to make it as profitable as movies. But Elvis was itching to get out in front of an audience and the receipts from the movies were now so poor that the Colonel could not refuse. He negotiated a deal in Vegas—$1 million for two weeks, two shows a night. It would prove the most successful show the city had ever seen.

Having again conquered Vegas, television, and radio, Elvis felt he had now reestablished himself sufficiently to take his show on the road. The Colonel booked him into a

They Died Too Young

grueling schedule of performances: 168 in 1971, 156 in 1972, and 169 in 1973, right across America. Clad in rhine-stone-encrusted stage suits, Elvis was thrilled to be in front of live audiences again, and albums of these live shows sold well. He even won a Grammy for the album *He Touched Me* in 1972.

With Elvis away on tour all the time, Priscilla would send him photographs of Lisa Marie and recordings of her first words to remind him he had a daughter. She was fed up with being cooped up at Graceland with his entourage, who made it obvious they did not like her, and she felt increasingly humiliated by his obvious interest in other woman.

She indulged in a brief affair with her dancing teacher, and then she took up karate (to try to share one of Elvis's interests) and fell in love with her tutor, Mike Stone. She knew her marriage was over. Painfully she plucked up courage to tell Elvis that she was leaving him and they were divorced on October 9, 1973. In the settlement she got $2 million, plus $10,000 a month in alimony and child support. Elvis bitterly threw a handful of money at her in court, saying that was all she had ever wanted, but by the time they got outside, they were holding hands.

The divorce affected Elvis badly, not because he particularly loved Priscilla anymore, but because she was the first woman who had left him for someone else. Physically he was shattered by the number of performances he was scheduled to give, and on stage he began to become a caricature of himself. All he had to do was be Elvis Presley to keep everyone happy, and gradually he began to lose track of himself in the myth.

In his famous 1973 concert in Hawaii, which was beamed around the world, he looked distracted, he had gained weight, and it was obvious that something was wrong. In fact Elvis was fed up and lonely, and increasingly paranoid about his personal safety. He carried guns wherever he went, and even wore a bulletproof vest on stage. He was also concerned about his health; he was diagnosed as having glaucoma in his left eye and he was convinced he was going blind.

Graceland after Priscilla's departure was very different. Many of Elvis's original gang had left, and his new entourage was made up of "yes men" who simply watched as he gorged himself on food and took more and more pills. Whatever city he was in, every concert was still a sellout, and it was as though he had no goals left. He had the windows at Graceland covered to block out the sunlight, and read spiritual books of every denomination, trying to find meaning in his success. He squandered his looks, his talent, his wealth, and no one was powerful enough, or perhaps cared enough, to stop him.

One brief moment of hope for Elvis came when Barbara Streisand approached him for the male lead in her film *A Star is Born*. Elvis was very excited about the project—at last, a role that would offer a challenge—and even checked in for a face lift in a Memphis hospital. However, the Colonel was furious that Barbara had contacted Elvis directly, and made sure the negotiations floundered, insisting that Elvis would be billed above Barbara. Eventually the role was given to Kris Kristofferson and Elvis was devastated.

Elvis spent the last two years of his life lonely and in pain. He had an enlarged heart, a twisted colon, a damaged kidney, and a serious prescribed-drug addiction. His weight soared to 250 pounds, he began to forget words on stage, and his performances bordered on self-parody.

Early in 1977 Elvis started dating Ginger Alden, Miss Memphis Traffic Safety 1976, who was twenty years his junior. Alden claimed that Elvis had asked her to marry him, but Elvis did not have enough time left to follow this through, even if it were true. By August he was completely lost and his sense of reality utterly distorted: he was incoherent and rambling and full of self-loathing.

On the last night of his life, he played racquetball at four

They Died Too Young

The memorial at Graceland

in the morning, as was usual, then went to bed to read while Ginger slept next to him. He called down to his aunt for some water and his medication at 6 A.M, saying he could not sleep. Ginger woke at 2 P.M., on August 16, 1977, to find him face down on the bathroom floor. The paramedics were called, and he was taken to Memphis Memorial Hospital, but all efforts to revive him failed.

The King of rock 'n' roll was dead, and the world could not believe it.

The body was taken to a Memphis funeral home, and laid out at Graceland the next day. Thousands of people paid their respects, and radio stations everywhere played his records back to back. The Colonel arrived from Palm Springs, and at the wake got Vernon to sign papers assigning the rights to manufacture Elvis-related products.

The coffin was first laid to rest at Forest Hill mausoleum next to Gladys, but when three masked men attempted to steal the body to try to prove the death had been faked, both coffins were quickly brought back to Graceland and buried in the meditation garden. An eternal flame was lit, and the following words were inscribed on Elvis's grave by Vernon: "He was a precious gift from God,/we cherished and loved dearly./He had a God given talent that he shared with the world."

Vernon died two years later, and was buried at Graceland next to his wife and son, who had "gone ahead to join Jesse." Elvis's entire fortune was left in trust to Lisa Marie, and in 1982 Colonel Parker was forced to relinquish all rights to the estate. To date, Elvis Presley's record sales exceed 1.5 billion.

INDEX

INDEX